THE PEREGRINE FALCONS OF YORK MINSTER

Carole Bromley is a York-based poet, teacher and editor. She has published three collections with Smith|Doorstop: *A Guided Tour of the Ice House* (2011), *The Stonegate Devil* (2015) and *Blast Off!*, a collection for children (2017). Carole is an Arvon tutor, a mentor for the Poetry Society, and a judge of many competitions. When not writing or teaching she loves walking and spending time with family – including her husband, four children and thirteen grandchildren.

The Peregrine Falcons
of York Minster

CAROLE BROMLEY

Valley Press

First published in 2020 by Valley Press
Woodend, The Crescent, Scarborough, YO11 2PW
www.valleypressuk.com

ISBN 978-1-912436-47-7
Cat. no. VP0167

A CIP record for this book is available from the British Library.

Cover and text design by Jamie McGarry.
Edited by Martha Sprackland.

Printed and bound in the EU by Pulsio, Paris.

Contents

Acknowledgements

Thanks are due to the editors of the following publications where some of these poems were first published: *The Rialto, Maligned Species Anthology* (Fair Acre Press, 2016), *Avis, The Everyday Poet* (Michael O'Mara Books, 2016), *The Interpreter's House, Picaroon, The High Window, Rat's Ass Review, Poetry News, Three Drops, Finished Creatures, Half Moon* (OWF, 2016), *Best of British* (Paper Swans, 2017), *New Boots and Pantisocracies* (Smokestack Books, 2015), *The Moth, The Emma Press Anthology of Love* (The Emma Press, 2015), *Verse Matters* (Valley Press, 2017), *Ink, Sweat and Tears, Poetry Salzburg, Poetry Shed, The Emma Press Anthology of Aunts* (The Emma Press, 2017), *One for the Road* (Smith|Doorstop, 2017), *This is Not Your Final Form* (The Emma Press, 2016), *Algebra of Owls, Valley Press Anthology of Yorkshire Poetry* (Valley Press, 2017) *Under the Radar, The Stanley Spencer Anthology* (Two Rivers Press, 2017), *Atrium, White Noise and Ouija Boards* (Three Drops, 2014), *The Hippocrates Prize Anthology* (Hippocrates Press, 2019), *The Hippocrates Book of the Heart* (Hippocrates Press, 2017), *Paper Swans Pocket Love Anthology* (Paper Swans, 2018*),* *Strix, Clear Poetry, Riggwelter, Noble Dissent* (Beautiful Dragons, 2018), *Body and Soul* (Whitelight Press, 2018), *Wells Poetry Competition Anthology 2014, Diversifly* (Fair Acre Press, 2018), *Ramingo's Porch, Coast to Coast to Coast, Second Place Rosette* (The Emma Press, 2018), *The North, Everything That Can Happen* (The Emma Press, 2019), *Whirlagust* (Yaffle Press, 2019), *The Result is What You See Today* (Smith|Doorstop, 2019), *Ten Poems about Snow* (Candlestick Press, 2019), *Well Versed, These are the Hands: An NHS Anthology* (Fair Acre Press, 2020), *An Insubstantial Universe* (Yaffle Press, 2020)

Some of the poems appeared in a pamphlet, *Sodium 136* (Calder Valley Poetry, 2019) and are published here with the kind permission of the editor.

'Emporium' was highly commended in the Open House Competition; 'All the pubs where we used to meet' won second prize in the Watermarks Writing Competition; 'Bumping into John Lennon' and 'Saltburn' won first and second prizes in the Poetry Space Competition 2017; 'Visiting Helen in the Afternoon' was commended in the NHS Award, 'Letter from Allan Bank' was highly commended in the 2019 McLellan Prize and 'First Year' was awarded the Poetry Society's Hamish Canham Award in 2019.

I would like to thank all my Arvon tutors, Peter and Ann Sansom, the York Stanza and Leeds University Poetry Group for help with these poems and also Jamie McGarry and Martha Sprackland at Valley Press.

for John, Tom, Jonathan, Helen and Katherine

Homing

All that morning it scratted
and crooned in its cage
under my desk,

brought in
as a visual aid
for Steven's hobbies talk.

At break I locked it in
with Danny's fishing flies
and Tom's mountain bike.

At lunchtime Steven came
with grain and water
and a soothing hand.

Last period he stood at the front,
his voice steady,
no trace of the stammer,

and explained about the ring
and the loft, how sometimes
they get blown off course

and all the time his hand
with its bitten nails
stroked the bird firmly.

At the end he led them out,
a small, skinny Pied Piper,
and released it.

Thirty-five upturned faces
watched till it disappeared
somewhere over New Earswick.

The Peregrine Falcons of York Minster

Best observed from Dean's Park
(bring binoculars and stand well back
so you don't get a crick in your neck),
Mr and Mrs Minster are high up
on the north-west tower,
on the balcony or on a grotesque.
The falcon prefers *The Thoughtful Man*
who for centuries has stroked his chin
and ignored the crowds below,
the tiercel sits on the eroded carving
the other side of the belfry –
the smaller of the two,
less powerful, more easy-going
with a neater and cleaner look
even when fluffed up and relaxing.
It's the female who hunts the pigeons
which nest on that ledge in Stonegate
just behind the stone cat above J. W. Knowles,
Stained Glass, Leaded Lights, Decorations.
Look out – the chicks will be
snatched and whisked to a nest
where the fledglings will soon take
their first scary flight from the House of God.

Red Kites at Harewood

They own the Yorkshire air, riding
its currents, shrugging off cold winds that bring
leaves rattling and children pedalling
on Boxing Day bikes, and couples hiking
hand in gloved hand, not looking
up at where they tremble on taut string

then stoop to snatch at carrion
or worms or sometimes a skittering
vole or a hedge sparrow foraging.
And now the low sun is dipping
behind the hill, trees are shivering,
birch and beech, Storm Conor's coming
and in their tops red kites are roosting.

Saltburn

August Bank Holiday and Elijah
wants to fly his kite. It's red and yellow
and shaped like a bird.
Plenty of wind and he soon gets the hang.
Run, says his dad, *keep running*
and he does. Running, running,
towards Redcar and the steelworks,
towards the town where his great-great-grandpa
built the whole High Street
and lived at number 129 from where
you could cut through to the beach
carrying a bucket for sea-coal.

But to Elijah, intent on keeping his kite aloft,
there's only this running, running
away from the pier and the cliff lift
and the flapping windbreak,
away from the candy-floss and ice cream,
away from the day trippers
towards the still winding gear
on his skinny, sparrow's legs,
the great bird casting its shadow
over the long, ribbed sands.

One of These Days

We really will turn out the loft.
There's an old pram in there gathering dust,
a suitcase of baby clothes, a ping-pong table,
those paper cranes Tom made in Japan.

Various wedding handbags in fuchsia,
emerald green and that black suede one
Jo's dad spilt gravy on while filling me in
on the big disappointments of his life.

I know there's still a tea chest from the move
and in it old love letters, that photo
of Rob smiling awkwardly at Caversham Lock
before the Head of the River Race.

Somewhere in there, too, is the wooden jeep
John made for the Action Men
with a bonnet that opens up
full of all the odd Sindy shoes.

I picture the last Action Man
dressed in the sweater Mum knitted,
propped back in the driving seat,
eagle eyes staring into the dark.

Jonathan

When you were smaller I was omniscient.
This morning I thought how I don't hear from you for weeks
and then, out of the blue, a text or a 5 a.m. phone-call —
that you're in danger, in a hospital in Canberra, about to be
    anaesthetised
so they can stop your heart and restart it. Or, last week, in a
    wooden chalet
on the shore of Lake Taupo in the path of Cyclone Cook
and I wanted to write a poem about how I put you at risk the day
I didn't tell the dentist I might be pregnant till after the X-ray
    and the time
I should have withdrawn you from the trip to Keswick but I
    didn't, just lay,
picturing the fallout from Chernobyl travelling on a strong wind
    towards you.

Departures

The day before you leave
you are suddenly kind.

You ring the removal firm
about shipping out the clock

the little table
that once stood in your gran's hall,

a blue bowl of pot pourri
where she'd bury the keys.

The petals have long faded
and smell only of dust.

You go into town to buy presents,
something expensive from Mulberry Hall,

a school of toy rabbits for Lotte.
Billy is more direct, misbehaving,

fretting about sweets for his cabin bag,
refusing to write his journal

runs back through security,
the airport like a funeral.

When you have gone

I look for solace in images:
you at Arrivals at 5 a.m.;

paddling in the memorial fountain,
then, in the shade, Jim asleep in your lap;

throwing a frisbee at Calke Abbey,
sharing a cold beer with Tom

barefoot in that yellow polo shirt,
on the beach, your gesture saying *It's nothing*;

queueing for the ferry at Southwold
all smiles in black cap and shades,

chasing crabs at Walberswick, laughing,
then Gun Hill at sunset, disconsolate

Today on FaceTime with Lotte –
at least she's learnt to chuck up in a bag –

you're clean-shaven in neatly pressed work-shirt,
your holiday beard down the plughole.

My mother's house

Smelt of washing, frying bacon,
talcum powder and warm milk.

My sister's smells of beagles,
manure and cardinal polish.

Mine, as far as I know, of baking bread,
of coffee, occasionally fish.

I could be wrong. My daughter-in-law
comments on my perfume,

how it clings to her daughter's hair.

Beverley Baths, 1959

I clung to the wall at the deep end
before launching my goose-pimpled body
into the bleachy water,
head determinedly aloft. How daft
to be afraid of something so beautiful.

Second attempt Avril swims beside me,
the rest of Form 1T cheering me on.
I'm eleven. I've never seen my parents
in swimsuits. How I dreaded Miss Atkinson
unhooking my clenched toes.

Sprint

I'm eleven though from my height
you might take me for thirteen,
wearing regulation navy-blue knickers
over my white 'linings'.
How they hamper me, hand-me-down baggy,
tucked-up like a kid in a storybook
fishing for tiddlers; and white Aertex shirt
greyed by the twin tub,
so shrunk it doesn't reach my waist.
I'm sporting a green band for Wenlock
but I'm not running for Wenlock.

I'm running for *me*. I'm running
for the joy of these long feet they rib me about.
Topper they call me because when I grow up
I want to be a Television Topper on the Band Show
and kick my long legs high in defiance
of Hawkeye who mocks my short 'a's,
who says when I move south people will *larf.*
I'm running. In my head I'm seeing how fast
I can thunder my feet on the track.
The hundred yards will be mine
and no one will laugh.

Flittin'

Today at the end of term service we say goodbye
to Oliver who starts a new school next term
and is very excited about his new house,
give him a round of applause,
watch the head teacher shake his small hand.

In six strange yards I wore the wrong colour,
wrong face, wrong accent. Even my words
were snatched from me and chucked
round the playground over my head:
clemmed, mardy, bairn, jammy, tarra.

I learnt to keep my gob shut till I knew
the new words, till my mum had scrimped
for the new uniform though I was allowed
to wear my good brown shoes out
among that alien sea of black leather.

Dinner was lunch now and tea was dinner
a butty was a sandwich, a bap a bread-bun
goodies were sweets and scran was grub
aye was yes and brass was money.
They laughed. I didn't find it funny.

Mash was brew and parky was cold,
there was no faffing now, no more larking
allus, summat and nowt were out
nobody offered me chuddy,
nobody gave me a croggy.

I was up-skelled, narky, vexed,
on a Scarborough warning
till I mastered this foreign tongue.
I wouldn't change places with Oliver.
Flit? Me? Not bloody likely. No ta.

Emporium

Dave Dee Shifts Things
it says over the door. And he does,
but not these things, it seems.
Not this plastic-covered chair,
the lost-looking occasional table,
the five matching wine glasses,
the floral gold-rimmed tea set
minus the teapot lid.
Baskets of ornaments and photos
from sad house clearances,
the Hummel figure with the glued-on foot,
the framed photograph of Rhyl,
a family in a porch. A utility sideboard
catches my eye, like the one we had
in Clarence Road, a drawer for fish forks
we never used, a cupboard
for the little jug of silver sixpences
that never got spent. I open the door
and feel in the gloom for that jug
that only came out at Christmas,
the Santa Claus custard jug
mum sent off for from Bird's,
that waited all year for its dusty corners
to be filled with hot, thick liquid
made from powdered egg and rum.

Message

My mother stopped being posh
when she was dying. I hoped
she might at last say she loved me
or just something nice. Anything.
Dialect or Standard English,
I really didn't mind just so long
as she meant it. I waited.
I waited for days. It didn't come.
She complained
and ordered people about
only now they didn't listen,
just went about their business
as kindly as they could.
I was still so afraid of her
that when she needed clothes
I went and bought new ones
rather than enter her house –
'Don't you dare go in my house
and mess everything up' –
and once when I arrived
the nurse on the desk said
'I was nearly sorry for her
on Thursday. I thought she was
dying but by Friday she was back
to her old tricks, ringing
that bloody bell'.

Wild Garlic

Your request, or so Di said.
Richard couldn't face it
so it was just the two of us

walking the riverbank
carrying what was left
of you. No bluebells,

just wild garlic, the reek of it
and no space either
without people.

Because it was horrific
like everything about that day,
because I had dropped you

in the car park, my hand shook
as I plunged it in
that hideous lucky dip

and could not cry, could not
think of you as you were,
only this imaginary you

who knew where bluebells grew,
the mother who was never wrong
blown hither and thither.

After

At first you think of her, your mother,
as she was just days before the funeral,
that afternoon she gripped your hand
and told you about her rings, her watch,
or the morning she would speak to no one
though you came and went with flowers.
You remember her hand, its veins,
the shocking whiteness of it,
the way, at the end, it seemed to claw you
after her. You think of her voice,
how it whispered that she
needed a bedpan though you knew,
because you could see it, she wore a pad.

You want to meet her
as she was when you were little,
go looking for her in all the old haunts.
You wish you still had that wedding dress
with forty-two covered buttons
your sister helped you into,
search attics, boxes, drawers
for old letters so she might speak to you.
Running a finger over her sepia face
is some comfort.

Finally, you search for the girl
before you knew her, imagine her meeting your father,
the way she might have covered her mouth
when she laughed, that discreet freshening
of the lipstick she once used. You make up
the name of it, *Red Sequin*, perhaps, or *Blaze*.

They go to see *Brief Encounter* at the Roxy,
run home hand in hand, laughing, through the rain.
Afterwards, an awkward hour in the parlour,
the fire, behind its guard, newly lit.

Ros's Frosty Strawberry Squares

I never make puddings. All my recipes,
my daughter says, are a bit retro. I flip through
the pages of the Good Housekeeping file
which would give any hygiene inspector a fit
and can see she has a point. Who would want
my mother's Bakewell Tart with its bossy p.s.
(food processors make super pastry!)
or my mother-in-law's neatly typed Gooseberry Pie,
Miss Parker's Lemon Pudding with a semi-colon
after each ingredient and the tops of all the letters missing.

The Sellotape's dried out and the column, snipped
from some posh broadsheet, flutters to the floor
with a seventies recipe for Pêches Brûlées
I don't remember making. And there, between
Coffee Crackle and Blender Pecan Pie,
I spot your familiar handwriting and I cry,
I cry for the days of Frosty Strawberry Squares,
for your brown ink, your neatly rounded 'a's
your '1 pkg. Dream topping', for the thought
of you in the old kitchen 'stirring occasionally'.

Between Santa Maria del Popolo and Black Moon

On the stamp a butterfly sips from a flower.
If I close one eye I can make out its name:
Argynnis adippe – the High Brown Fritillary.

I recognise your neat, rounded handwriting at once
though I don't remember receiving the card
from *such a modern, curious and imaginative city.*

I know you would have delighted in the stamp
as you delighted in Barcelona, too,
not knowing what was taking hold.

In fact your thoughts were all for *A who has been ill
the last few weeks but seems so much better*
and for me and my family, *especially Elijah.*

He was a baby then – five now – and you in your grave
these two years. I picture you handing over
65 céntimos for the stamp, near the Sagrada Familia,

those extraordinary spires reaching
towards an already darkening sky.

On the Death of a Friend in Childhood

after Donald Justice

I will never meet you grey and toothless
in a heaven I no longer believe in
or in a hell where you did not belong.

Some instinct was it stopped me weeping
until I could be alone, until I could close the door
and lie down and grieve on my own.

Friday on the bus home we'd joked
about Beaky and the skirt your mum was making,
camel with a claret-coloured top

that you would never wear. By Monday
you were dead from blood poisoning
and I was learning not to make a fuss

but hold it in all day and chant French verbs
and try to eat mashed potato with parsley
and ride home beside a stranger.

Visiting Helen in the Afternoon

i.m. Helen Cadbury 1965–2017

I have washed my hands before
the first set of doors,
sanitised them before the second,

I have passed the dying,
their oxygen, their drips,
their hushed visitors and found you here,
still you, giddy from Oromorph.

You tell me you get Byron now
and I joke that he had bowel trouble too
or was that Coleridge,

though I don't feel like joking,
what I feel like is hugging.
What I feel like is running a mile.

We play the denial game
though afterwards I wonder
was this kind of me, or cowardly?

You say on steroids the ideas
for stories just keep coming,
one every minute. You make notes
so they don't escape.

You worry that I've cycled without a helmet,
I worry I may have stayed too long.
You look at the patch of blue,

the white clouds at the top of the window
where the glass isn't frosted
and say 'that's the real world,
my own bit of it, everything blue and clear.'

Friend's Burial Ground

i.m. Helen Cadbury

It was a nice touch to have the guy tell us
why we were there, like a train guard;
If you do not intend to travel, leave the train now.

It's all getting a bit Wicker Man,
Dave said when the little girl played the recorder.
I made a note of the gap in the hedge.

A bird flew overhead, wheeled across
Walmgate Stray at the moment of silence
before they lowered you.

What were you thinking when you chose
'Over the Rainbow', the notes so high I can't reach them
even when I'm not trying not to cry?

The rosemary passed round in the basket
clung to my fingers. As if I'd forget.

Messengers

One day you'll get a phone call
or a policeman will come knocking.
You'll look out of the window
and the trees, roses, birds
will have changed.

It will be a new country
where you don't speak the language.
You'll need a glass of water,
great painful gulps of it,
to speak at all.

You will stare at your feet
as if they don't belong to you,
as if you have forgotten how to take
a step. Suddenly you will know
what it is to be old.

A storm is coming. I feel it
in my wrist. The dog at the sea's edge
senses it, worries at the tide
as though he could make it turn,
leaving the white shore clean.

The D Word

My daughter avoids talking about it.
Her daughter is too young for it.
The little girl who strangled herself
on her first day at nursery
was just very poorly. The same nursery,
the same slide with the same rope
someone should have noticed
that my granddaughter had been down
a hundred times, was taken away
brick by smashed brick and smoothed over,
talked about only
in whispers or words mouthed by adults.
Today she drips water
into the mouth of a dying hamster
like someone who knew all along.

Songs of Praise

A man kneels on the earth floor
and prays to Gabriel for his life.

He is on the very edge of Europe.
Once we camped there

waiting for a ferry and the kids
dug holes with seaside spades

and all night the lighthouse beam
swept our canvas house.

The interviewer asks if it is right
to try to enter a country illegally

and the student priest replies
with courtesy that it is not

but what are we supposed to do?

I Had Forgotten the Cats

How innocent we were,
contemplating the Acropolis,
yet more concerned with the kittens
that prowled begging on its stones.
Looking through the album
I'm surprised to see them.
It's as though someone
had placed them in our hands
for the shot, like the puppies
they posed the kamikaze pilots with
before they wrote the letter home,
before they wet the bed,
before they climbed into the cockpit
with just enough petrol
to reach the ships.

The Dark Soft Languages are Being Silenced

(Margaret Atwood)

The vast landmass of Australia
is marked with a thousand dots,
each black one pinpointing the spot
where a language fell silent:
Maya, Miwa, Djangun, Yatay,
each red one the severely endangered:
Kartujarra with five speakers,
Wanggamala just one.

I picture him, an old man under a scribbly-gum,
talking to himself, keeping alive
the word for the angle of a spear,
the depth of a waterhole.
No one is listening. His wife who once sat
with him under a thousand stars died years ago.
White men with a machine came
to take away his voice.

He shook his head, the beads in his hair jangling
when they asked him if he could write.

My Case

Its abandoned doppelgänger
goes round and round on the carousel
long after the crowds have gone.
I curse myself for not tying on
a sparkly Christmas ribbon,
for not painting a Union Jack on it
like we did on our tortoise.

I walk through *Nothing to declare*
and out into bright sun, in my hand a passport,
Ted Hughes: The Unauthorised Life,
a banana, crisp new euros in a purse
I never use, and sunglasses.
I hail a taxi, feeling oddly weightless,
my knickers gone, my six ironed T-shirts.

Bumping into John Lennon

The signature specs had gone,
he had that myopic, sore-eyed peer
all contact-lens wearers have.

He'd ditched the white robes
and had a crew cut. I bought him a drink
and I think it was a relief to talk.

He told me it had become a bit much,
that he couldn't keep up all that showering.
She got most of the money. He started again,

took a City and Guilds in woodwork,
started a business doing sash windows.
He showed me the scar. A flesh wound.

He had an allotment, loved cycling,
would set off every Sunday at five a.m.
in fluorescent Lycra.

Once or twice he crept into the back
of Macca's concerts but, to be honest,
couldn't take the hair dye, the lyrics.

The last time I saw him
he was up a ladder fixing a pane,
whistling 'Maxwell's Silver Hammer'.

Cambridge Entrance

Why would you like to live on the moon?
'You have two hours'
My mind was a blank, round and white.

The other girl's pen set off
like a rocket; mine was grounded.
Counting down to zero.

She must have seen the moon
as a fine nail paring. Mine was fat,
the man having a laugh.

I never wanted to live alone.
I made my one small step
out of that room.

Uncle Arnold

He lived by the river. There were stepping stones
and a tabby cat that jumped across them
to greet me. We'd go fishing with jam jars
and pieces of string. We'd be out all day
till he called us in by banging a spoon on a tin.

Uncle Arnold made everything out of tins.
He seemed to choose them at random
from that stone shelf in his deep, inexhaustible pantry.
There had been an Aunt Isabel but that was before my time.
Maybe she had an opinion about the tins.

Of course it wasn't like that. We never went there.
I only knew about Arnold from whisperings
before my dad took the train to Durham on Saturdays
and afterwards never told us where he'd been.

In Praise of the Stinging Nettle

Once we dyed our clothes with it,
drank it as a potion for rheumatics,
gathered it for puddings, beer and soup.

Where would the larvae of the peacock butterfly,
the tortoiseshell, dot moth, mouse moth, ghost moth
be without the underside of its soft, hairy leaves?

This plant that loves damp, thrives in meadows,
springs up round derelict buildings,
is not welcome in our tidy borders

but leave just one clump in a corner
and your garden will be filled with butterflies
while the songbirds who take them serenade you.

Old Mother Shipton

Outside her cave on petrified ropes
an ice skate, a teddy bear, a sock –

witch or prophetess, tourists still queue
to dip their hand in her well.

On her grave outside York:
Here lies she who never lied.

Her prophecies came true,
iron ships and flying machines.

Her mother was a dangerous woman,
fifteen and pregnant, gave birth

in a cave, refused to name the father,
was taken away to a convent.

The daughter with the hooked nose
never saw her again but lived in the woods

ignoring kids who threw stones
and hanging up their mittens like washing.

Chagall in Bornacoola

It's December and Chagall strolls
down the high street
to the Coach and Horses
which is, as it transpires,
disappointingly deserted,
the chairs uncomfortable,
losing some of their straw.
The beer is satisfyingly cold though.
Chagall orders another pint
and peers at a flurry of snow
through a corner of the window
where the stained glass is missing.
He wonders about
the buoyancy of water
when it's frozen. A couple
walk by, hand in hand,
laughing, the girl catching snow
on her tongue, the boy
taking advantage of the moment
to kiss her long and deep.
Chagall drains his glass,
fetches another and falls asleep
dreaming of the couple
rising, floating above the town
where a tractor turns to slush
the snow that has settled on the road.

A breath

We can't say they didn't warn us.
The path is beautiful but treacherous

but we go anyway, slithering and falling
through the woods and up the rutted track

where the air is suddenly cold
and so sharp it takes our breath away,

and we're too busy admiring the view
to give a thought to getting back

through the gathering dark, our signals dead,
to the meal already on the table.

I think of all snowy moments the best

must have been that moment
on Shackleton's makeshift sledge

three men on mats of coiled rope
launched over the precipice into

a future that could have been death –
the 3,000 foot descent, the shredded breeks

and then the distant steam whistle
from the whaling station

calling them in from snow and ice that kill
but also are beautiful and draw you

across crisp untouched miles –
that moment when the first voice cried

Wheeeeeee

Snow

after Don Paterson

I hate all films that start with snow,
Christmas schmaltz the lot of them:
Bambi, Love Story, Frozen.

The cynical director, his assistant
with the snow machine
blowing flakes

to muffle the cries of motherless fawn,
orphaned little girls in castles,
a young wife breathing her last.

I've nothing against a good cry
and I'll make an exception
for *Doctor Zhivago* and the ice palace

where Yuri will make a fresh start
despite the wolves, will write poems
in fingerless gloves, ice on his moustache,

even though I know it won't end well,
that she'll step into the fur-lined sleigh,
that he'll breathe a hole in the ice for one last look.

I have been thinking

of the spider in the printer in the barn
who must have taken refuge
deep inside its workings
having sensed my approaching feet
or perhaps the rain drumming on the roof
that still leaks in the far corner.

I wonder what his last thoughts were
when the green light went on
and the ticking began
and the cheap white paper
started to roll in the darkness
and there was nowhere left to run.

I will never have the chance now
to ask him for his thoughts on that draft
of a poem called 'A Girl's Head'
which slowly emerged from the slot
with its laser-sharp letters
and two of his eight articulated legs.

Declaration

I am a poem. Do not tie me to a chair
and demand answers. I am innocent.
I can only scream.

I am a poem. Do not ask me to win back
your lost lover. I have my own problems.
Are you listening?

I am a poem. Do not expect me
to bring back your father from the dead.
I am not Jesus.

I am a poem. Do not come to me
for stand-up. I am not
a pantomime horse.

I am a poem. Do not invite me
to your stupid cocktail party.
I hate small talk.

I am a poem. Do not offer me
walking boots and a compass.
I am the mountain.

Letter from Allan Bank

Oh Mama, I had the strangest dream. The house was on fire
and William propped up in bed. I shouted but no words came.
Woke up and there she was in the doorway, finger on lips, smiling.

It's so cold! No wonder William never liked this house.
Dorothy's still here, giving him those weird looks.
She took to her bed on our wedding day,

wore my ring all the night before. It was still warm
when he slipped it on my finger. When he came to ask
for my hand, her cold pork was still in his pocket!

She walks into Ambleside every day without fail,
tapestry bag under her arm, to fetch the post. And she bakes.
Cakes and more cakes. Not a tooth in her head.

Aunt Reed

I hated the sickly, whining, pining thing.
I'd have sooner have been charged
with a pauper brat out of a workhouse.

I'd enough of my own.
Eliza and Georgiana to marry off
and John such a handful.

Mostly I left Jane to the servants,
couldn't stand the sight of her.
That book was the last straw.

How was I to know there'd be typhoid?
She got her comeuppance
with that sign round her neck.

And I wasn't about to lend a hand
in lifting her to prosperity,
not after the things she said.

Cruel? Give me strength. I was *kind*.
She'd have starved without me,
she'd have ended up on the streets.

Some people don't know they're born.

Betsey Trotwood

I wanted a niece not a nephew.
I make no bones about that. Swung my bonnet
at the idiot doctor when he told me.
Had to take the jewellers' cotton out of my ears;
I'd stuffed them to shut out the screams.
Silly girl was a baby herself. I left her to it,
just walked out and never came back.

Went home to chase donkeys off my grass
and look after Mr Dick. He was a baby too
with his giant kite. Still, after David turned up
ten years later like an urchin on my step
and called me *Aunt* I made up for it.
Oh Lord, I said, *what shall we do with him?*
and Mr Dick said *Give him a bath.*

Hetty Sorrel

The moon is full and soon the stars will appear,
though here they are different stars.

The gum trees are a blur, golden in what's left of the sun.
How relentless it is, how it parches the land.

I lie awake and dream of lush meadows, of cows grazing;
here the sheep are skin and bone.

In two more years I can go home
though I doubt there will be a place for me.

Sometimes I watch lovers on the hard ground,
a sailor with a wife back home, a girl who was caught

stealing stockings or a rose-coloured ribbon
and remember Arthur Donnithorne,

the warmth of his arms before I knew
what treachery was. Sometimes I watch a child

under the southern sun, her white dress,
her bonnet, up to her knees in golden grass,

her white underthings drying on that line tied
between tent and tree.

I never meant for the baby to die. I tucked it in
to the roots of an oak, covered it with a blanket of twigs

and walked away. All night its cries reached me,
they still reach me under the great grave sky.

'Red cloth and epaulets'

Her favourite poem was Lalla Rookh
so Rosamond Vincy wove her dreams
and went forth to greet the King of Bukhara
only to bump into a poet
whose songs were so sweet
she swooned away and found alas
king and poet are not always the same.

The business of her life was furniture,
her aim to fill her married home
with silver and plate and baubles,
polished tables, gilded mirrors
which did not bring out her pretty smile,
only reflected how she saw herself
when accomplishments were not enough.

Charlotte Brontë's Paintbox

It smells of sandalwood and oil,
of ancient charcoal and lead.
If it could talk it would speak
in a conspiratorial whisper.
Worn smooth by small white hands,
her prints still here on its dark interior.
If I put my lips to it, I could taste
the printing ink on the lid.
It looks like my granny's sewing box
with its neat drawers and ledges,
or the Japanese musical box
my grandfather gave me, a key
for each secret compartment,
the paint still yellow in its little pot.

The New Mother

found poem from Every Woman's Doctor Book

If your figure is not as trim as before
make yourself a brassiere
from a 45-inch length of towelling.

Most mothers whose figures are loose
will be much improved
by wearing a good corset belt.

If there are obvious rolls of fat
in the stomach wall you will need
a controlling under-belt.

Have a daily sponge-down or tepid bath
and give every inch of your body
a brisk towelling afterwards.

Sufferers from falling hair
can take a general tonic such as
Easton's Syrup or Parrish's Chemical Food.

The tissues are relaxed and tender
for a month after a baby is born
and especially when stitches have been needed.

It is wise to wait for six weeks.
I have known instances where married lives
have been rendered miserable.

Writing Desk

I found it in a junk shop in Bishy Road;
the label said *Lady's Writing Desk*.

So pretty with its red leather top,
its slim, turned legs, drawer with brass catch.

A man would need to spread himself,
his important work laid out around him

while I perch on a cushioned lady's chair
writing poems with a lady's fountain pen.

But it's worm-eaten, my desk, rough to the touch.
I run my fingers over fragile tunnels,

find little piles of fine sand in the drawer
on my pencils, my ruler, my hole punch

where creatures have burrowed out and flown
into the stairs, the floors, the rafters.

Gwen John

Have you got a brother, Puss?
Do you sometimes wish you hadn't?
Augustus Pussycat. A fine name.
Do you like it when I stroke you like that?
I envy you your simple life:
fish, milk, sleep, paw-washing.

Nothing makes me purr like painting
my studio or women sideways on
or, sometimes, Puss, the likes of you.
You're very handsome, did I tell you that?
I told Monsieur Rodin he was beautiful
but he just went on sculpting *The Kiss*.

Now he's returning my notes,
cutting me in the street.

She should have christened me Augusta
after herself. Augusta John.
That would have made them sit up.

People of the future, can you hear me?
Is it true they call Augustus
'brother of the more famous Gwen?'

Chance Meeting

We were two strangers on a train.
I got on at Reading, he at Slough
and, though I doubt we'll ever meet again,

I can recall that conversation even now.
It was so natural, as if he knew
the thoughts that I was trying not to show.

There's something about meeting someone new
that makes me suddenly intimate.
I loved that poem, I said, *didn't you?*

pointing to it in a supplement
which lay before us on the table.
I'll take that as a compliment,

he said, *perhaps I ought to wear a label.*

Time

I will rest on the wrist of a woman
who barely glances at me
warmed by the thud
of her pulse. At night I'll lie alone
looking at the ceiling, knowing
she'll turn back to me on waking,
that she relies on my unchanging face,
the way my hands move in the dark.

Go ahead, I'm listening

Have you ever been in love?
That's an interesting question, Carole.
What would you do if you were me?
This isn't about me, it's about you.
What kind of answer is that?
That's another interesting question.
I can't sleep. What should I do?
Have you tried counting electric sheep?
Do you always answer a question with a question?
That's another interesting question.
You should be a psychotherapist.
Interesting idea.
What time is it in Sydney, Siri?
Midday. Is there anything else I can help you with?

One More Frozen Orange Juice

I do not remember the name of the park
where you rowed me across the lake,
only the pink dress I was wearing.

I have totally forgotten what the building
was called that you said was phallic –
I didn't know what the word meant.

Don't ask me your room number in High Hall
which has no doubt been demolished.
We could see the whole of Birmingham from that bed.

First Year

Oh, Tom, I'm wearing my lucky pants in the reading room
but you still turn away. Come back. I'd like one night with you.
I'd like every slow day in your arms. I can't read this Bible;
I'm taking my time but the lines run away into the rain.
I'm a cat on an ice box longing to touch your hair.

Nothing I love is rubbish

after The Lovers (The Dustman) *by Stanley Spencer*

My hair is grey but you made it beautiful
with your dirty fingers. When I look back on our love
nothing is discarded, not the cracked red teapot,
not the empty jam tin, not the cabbage stalks.

Take these mucky cord trousers, held up with string.
They were everything. Take my spotted shirt,
too big for the arms that held you; or this enamel jug
that dangles from my hand.

O, my grubby love, how I dream of you,
of your weary, soiled body which I will carry
past the picket fence, the clipped peacock, the white dog,
the broken crockery, the green feathers of my old hat

towards the open cottage door,
that glint of firelight, those tied-back curtains,
the stone lintel, the latticed window,
the man with the beard who is always looking up.

The Word

The worst thing is not remembering
what word it was made her turn aside.

How lovely her eyelashes, how lustrous her hair,
the way her hips swayed, carrying the jug.

I fell in love with the soil between her brown toes,
with the sky above that small moving figure.

I was a crazy man, crazed by that loveliness,
thirsting for the clean water slopping from the rim.

The world was rich with words, like a laden fig tree
and I reached out my clumsy hand.

Heart

How is your heart, my love, without me?
Does it form the old figure of eight?
Does it have that pumpernickel smell?
Once we were melting custard,
hot and sweet and full of tears.

Oh the hubble-bubble of it
under that eiderdown.
My heart has forgotten you.
Forgive me. I write fast about what hurts
because I cannot bear the ordinary hiss and tick.

Tell me, from that space you know inside yourself,
how is your heart without me?

Rathke's Cleft Cyst

Strange to think you were part of me,
that I carried you with me always
like an April fool that wasn't funny
or one of those burry weeds
I used to throw at my grandad's back.

Strange to think of you piggy-backing
while I played leapfrog in Clarence Road,
jeered at Creambun from across the dyke,
had disturbing dreams about Victor,
changed school seven times,
learnt to be invisible, to do without
a best friend since they were all taken.

Strange to think you were there
when I queued for Beatles tickets
and that policeman said *Now, now
don't get hysterious,*
there when I read my finals results
and hadn't the heart to ring my mother.

Stranger still to think
of four labours with you tucked
underneath my brain
wondering when would be
a good time to start growing.

Strangest of all that you were there
when I sat at my desk writing
that first poem that I was afraid
to show anyone, like I might get arrested.
You were there in all those pubs,
there when I took up smoking.

Afterwards

Make a fist for me.
Now, push your heel against my hand.
Now pull my fingers towards you.

How is it I forgot this
when I remembered the words
Do you know where you are?

She tells me it's so she can compare.
Afterwards. I had not thought,
really thought, of afterwards

only of an end to the pain,
the way the ward is blurred,
the endless, endless nausea.

So matter of fact. Afterwards.
It isn't logical but I want to say
My brain is a long way from my feet.

Holding Bay

Lonely as Tucker Murphy,
sole Bermudan athlete,
in the Opening Ceremony
of the Winter Olympics
which I've been parked in front of
while I wait to be operated on.
Isn't it exciting says the nurse
as the cross-country skier
dances past the cameras
in scarlet shorts.

Neurosurgery Ward 4 Bed 8

The drain in my spine is emptied: 10 mls
of brain fluid per hour. The nurse appears
to turn the tap. If I sit up the headache worsens

so I lie flat under my regulation cotton blanket
and, for hours, watch the pigeons dance on the rooftop
where sometimes a man appears to tie down the net.

The nurses tell me it's windy but nothing moves,
there are no trees or reeds to whisper in the wind.
How determined they are, my pigeons,

to make their nest in this inhospitable place.
It must be warm on top of the air conditioners
and behind, if the man would only let them,

they could bring twigs and mate and lay warm eggs
and preen themselves in privacy and warmth.
How I would like to preen myself. In three more days

I can shower and wash my hair. I can cut my nails.
How determined they are, my beautiful pigeons.
If only the man in grey would leave them alone.

I want to fling open the window and let in the air
and call out to them, *Thank you. Thank you*
thank you, thank you, my beautiful birds.

Visiting Time

In here everyone talks to the dead.
Some speak aloud, Barry calls to his son;
Enid, who, after having her hip done
broke the other one getting out of bed,
talks to her late husband, telling him
This is the worst pain and I'm not joking
and I, inside my head, talk to my mum
which is ironic as we barely spoke.

I'm sorry I didn't buy you the dressed
crab that awful lunchtime. You guessed,
as I did not, it would be your last,
afterwards you'd eat little and then less
then not even sips out of a beaker,
just me wielding the sponge on a stick.

To My Cyst

Flu set you going
like a ticking bomb,
growing, growing
in the cramped space
between skull and brain
which I imagine
as like a crack in a tunnel
where a buddleia
tries to flourish.
You see them from trains,
that urge to grow,
or mushrooms in a shed.
You had food and water;
you would make it.
I was your host,
me, this me that cries
and loves and is typing
these black letters
on infinite space.

Meditation on Fear

It's only now I am afraid.
At the time I was both in it
and above it, thinking, all too aware
that people close to death
feel as though they are floating
above their own body.
I was curious. I am a writer
and it saved me. I had a notebook
David brought in and a biro.
When I was admitted I thought
All those months and no poems
for the Hippocrates Prize
and today is the deadline,
what terrible timing. That is
what part of me was thinking,
the rest of me was feeling
and that's a different thing altogether.
Then when they kept telling me,
waving those pink forms in my face,
that I could die or have a stroke
or wake up blind, I said
I am a writer. The first line
of my poem will be Blindness,
Stroke, Death and I trusted them
and we laughed about it.
I am not brave. I had no choice.
And there were moments in the night
I would not like to revisit
and all day I was terrified
but it's good being a writer,
even when they parked me
in front of that obscene TV

while they sharpened their instruments
to open my skull, my eyes
were following that lone athlete
which could have been the last
thing I saw and my mind
which they could have destroyed
was thinking *If I get out of here alive*
that will make a great metaphor.